Even More

Inspirations of God

by

Jerry Barfield

R.D. Talley Books
Bookstore & Publishing

www.rdtalleybooks.com

Las Vegas, Nevada

The Holy Bible version referenced in this book is the King James Version.

ISBN: 978-1-957294-18-6

R.D. Talley Books Publishing, LLC
4882 W. Lone Mountain Rd.
Las Vegas, Nevada 89130
www.rdtalleybooks.com

Table of Contents

Introduction

Three times God has stirred up the gift that He has given me, to use His word to not only lift up His name, but to lift up my brothers and sisters so that their joy may be restored. We know that in our walk each day, we get barraged by Satan's imps. And that's exactly what they are; small things that we can trample and put under our feet.

I thank God for what He has given me to obtain all power and glory for Him. I pray that as you read this, you will perceive this word, receive His word and conceive the gift within you and that you proceed with the mission that will allow the world to believe in Him.

Thank you and God bless!

Power

Matthew 28:18

"And Jesus came and spake unto them saying, 'All power is given unto me Heaven and in Earth.'"

Power: the one thing for centuries mankind has been trying to achieve successfully for only a season, or to end in death. Mankind has been willing to lie, cheat, steal, hurt or even kill in their thirst for power. The power that Esau and Jacob fought for, even in the womb of Rebekah. The power that had Herod searching his kingdom for the baby named Jesus, and it was that same power that Pharaoh tried to hold over the people of Israel before giving it to Moses and so many other moments!

Power is defined from the Latin word *posse*, meaning to be able; (1) ability to act; capability and (2) the right, ability, or capacity to exercise control; legal authority. Both Moses and Paul were working under the "authority" of God. Moses had been instructed, according to Exodus 9:16, with God saying, *"And in very deed for this cause have I raised thee up, for to shew in thee my power; and that my name may be declared throughout all the earth."* That was to show Pharaoh what God can do through Moses about power.

And with Paul, when he wrote with joy and never hiding it at any time in Romans 1:16; *"For I am not ashamed of the gospel of Christ: for it is the power of God unto salvation to everyone that believeth; to the Jew first, and also to the Greek."*

That is the type of power that we receive when we take God into our lives. But God gives to us gifts that are to be used to His glorification and nothing else. When we let Jesus Christ truly live in our lives, He allows us to have power. Not just any power, but three different types of power that it will be fully used to the glory of our Lord, Jesus Christ.

1. **We have the power of healing**. We know that healing is a gift as well, but there are other types of healing than of the body, which is important. But all who have taken Jesus Christ have this type of healing, to heal minds, hearts and especially souls to give in the service of God. In Hosea 6:1 it says, *"Come, and let us return unto the Lord: for he hath torn, and he will heal us; he hath smitten, and he will bind us up."* We were God's from the start, but were separated from Him by sin. It's only by the blood of Christ that we are able to return to God to be healed by His grace and mercy.

2. **We have the power of life**, for Psalms 27:1 tells us that, *"The Lord is my light and my salvation; whom shall I fear? The Lord is the strength of my life; of whom shall I be afraid?"* Since we have taken Christ, we have a new life, where the very source of that life is Jesus. While we walk in this world, we in turn can give life once again to others by telling them all about the one that gives life and gives it freely, Jesus Christ!

3. **We have the power of love**. Psalms 91:14 lets us

know of this great and excellent love: *"Because he hath set his love upon me, therefore will I deliver him: I will set him on high, because he hath known my name."* It's because of this final power that we can truly overcome each and every obstacle that the devil tries to put against us, and we in turn can share these powers because without the third power, the first two can never work the way God intended for them to work. A kind word, a gentle smile, an understanding heart, a compassionate touch and many other things that brings out your healing powers to those who truly need them can bring forth life, and it all stems from love that God has shown us. In return, we can show it to others and that truly is power!

Hoping and Waiting

Lamentations 3:26

"It is good that a man should both hope and quietly wait for the salvation of the Lord."

Salvation, in the sense of those that have taken Jesus Christ as Lord and Savior, indeed is a good thing. Not just a good thing but the greatest thing that has ever happened. It's so great that we want to share it with others all around us because of the excitement that it gives and the joy that salvation gives in our lives.

Salvation comes from the Latin word *Salvus*, meaning safe. Proverbs 29:25 tells us, *"The fear of man bringeth a snare: but whoso putteth his trust in the Lord shall be safe."* I believe that explains itself. Salvation means (1) the process or state of being saved. Romans 10:9 says, *"that if thou shalt confess with thy mouth the Lord Jesus, and shalt believe in thine heart that God hath raised him from the dead, thou shalt be saved."*

(2) Deliverance from sin and penalty, realized in a future state. Romans 10:10 tells us, *"For with the heart man believeth unto righteousness; and with the mouth confession is made unto salvation"*, but in order to have salvation, you have to confess and believe in Jesus' name. John 3:18 tells us, *"He that believeth on him is not condemned: but he that believeth not is condemned already, because he hath not believed in the name of the only begotten Son of God."*

(3) And means of deliverance from danger, evil or ruin. There are quite a few people in which this meaning pertains to, people such as Joseph, Moses, etc. who had been delivered in one way or another by God's hand, just as we were. When we were out in the world not doing God's will, there were people in our lives hoping and waiting for us, but it took time. Just as Paul said in 1 Corinthians 3:6, *"I have planted, Apollos watered; but God gave the increase."* Someone planted the seed of salvation in your heart and then God sent another, or others, to water to give that seed life, but it is truly God that will give the increase of the fruit we bear in our lives to others for the glory of God.

And just like the seed that is planted, it took hoping and waiting for that seed to grow into a tree. It will that same kind of hoping and waiting for us to grow into the kind of people God wants us to be. So, just as someone was hoping and waiting for our salvation, now it's our turn to be doing the same for others to show them God's salvation, and also, to be hoping and waiting!

Heart Knowledge

Psalms 119:11

"Thy word have I hid in mine heart, that I might not sin against thee."

Think about it; when we want to keep something dear, something precious, something or someone close to us, we put them close to our hearts because of how much we love them. When we took Jesus in our lives, we put Him in our heart and that is where we put His word as well, because we love to see and hear His word also in our hearts and allow it to touch our hearts as well.

"Thy word", which is God's word, is total truth and has no lie in it. It gives us power, wisdom, understanding, joy, peace, etc., but the best thing about His word is that it's our guide in the darkness of sin. Psalms 119:105 tells us, *"Thy word is a lamp unto my feet, and a lamp unto my path."* It helps us each and every day to see Christ in a sin-darkened world.

"Have I hid in mine heart". When man receives knowledge from man, it goes to his head to use in time as wisdom, but when man receives knowledge from God, it goes to his heart. It's the heart that God looks at first and foremost, for that is where any of our true intents are. Jeremiah 24:7 lets us know that God said, *"And I will give them a heart to know me, that I am the Lord: and they shall be my people, and I will be their God: for they shall return unto me with their whole heart."*

Once we know God first and foremost in our hearts, we can keep His love, joy, peace and all that He gives to us in our hearts while knowing that it's in a safe place. That way, we may receive the knowledge that He gives to us to live out our lives for God and Him alone.

"That I might not sin against thee." We are prone to sin and we do it without any thought and the conviction of the Holy Spirit. Proverbs 28:13 lets us know that, *"He that covereth his sins shall not prosper: but whoso confesseth and foresaketh them shall have mercy."* Not only that, but Romans 3:23 explains to us that, *"For all have sinned, and come short of the glory of God."* But the good news about it is in Romans 3:24: *"Being justified freely by his grace through the redemption that is in Christ Jesus:"*.

Because of the redemption of Jesus, we can have a one-to-one relationship with God. Through that relationship, God can share His love with us and for us to share that love to others, and that truly is heart knowledge!

He's Closer Than You Think!

Jeremiah 23:23

"Am I a God at hand, saith the Lord, and not a God afar off?"

This is what God said through His prophet Jeremiah to let the false prophets know that He is the true and living God; the same one that created heaven and earth, the one who delivered the Hebrews out of Egypt, the one who caused the heavens to open up and rain for forty days and forty nights, and afterwards made a covenant with His people with a rainbow! This same God who hears, sees and knows all. Even when we think he doesn't, he does. The same one we, like Jeremiah had done, cry out to when we don't feel His presence, hear His voice or feel His touch. Not just in our lives, but in our hearts as well!

God knows what's going on in our lives, even when we don't even begin to understand, see what we will do or where we stand. It's always when we think when things are going wrong that we want to talk with God. Can't we do it when everything is going good as well? We know that it's hard, but I'm sure that God will show us that as well.

You just don't have to be in church to find God, but it's a start. David had said in Psalms 133:1, *"Behold, how good and how pleasant it is for brethren to dwell together in unity."* Not just the unity of others, who have received God in their lives and believe what Jesus Christ had done for them in their lives, but the unity that we have with God.

That is the most important thing that we can ever have!

So, as we are in our church, home, job or anywhere else that we may be at, God will be with you to do the work that He has for you. And when you feel that He isn't there, don't worry. It will be alright! Why? Because He's closer than you think!

Nothing Is Impossible to God

Jeremiah 32:27

"Behold, I am the Lord, the God of all flesh: is there any thing too hard for me?"

This is what is known as a rhetorical question and a rhetorical question is a question put only for oratorical or literary effect. The answer being implied in the question is a simple one. But this isn't just any man asking this question. It's God himself asking this question through the prophet Jeremiah.

We can look at this question and can only give one answer, and that answer being no. But why does God ask this question? Because of the fact that the world still does not believe, or refuses to believe, that there is a God and that He holds the answer to each and every man and woman's question. All we have to do is let Jesus Christ into our hearts, lives and souls and to allow Him to take proper reign in these areas!

This question has also been asked in Genesis 18:14, when God spoke to Abraham saying, *"Is any thing too hard for the Lord? At the time appointed I will return unto thee, according to the time of life, and Sarah shall have a son."* This is the same God who made life in an empty womb, who caused the Red Sea to part, who allowed His son to be conceived by a virgin, to heal the sick and the lame, who is able to reunite a family by His love and grace.

Is there anything too hard for God? The real answer comes out of Jeremiah 32:17 while being imprisoned saying, *"Ah Lord God! Behold, thou hast made the heaven and the earth by thy great power and stretched out arm, and there is nothing too hard for thee."* If it was that simple to see it then, why can't we see that now? But as long as you let God work it out, then you will see that nothing is impossible to God!

To Know Him Is To Trust Him

Hosea 4:1

Too many times we search out for truth, trust and love, but we really look for is trust. Trust is one thing we really don't have enough or a lot of, but when we have a better knowledge and understanding of an issue or subject, we automatically have trust. That's what happens when we take Jesus in our lives, for He put the trust and love of God into our hearts.

And how do we know Him? The answer is as simple as the nose upon your face: we begin to know Him by reading and learning His word, which will enlighten and educate us to God and what He has for us in this life and has chosen for us to live for His glory. The prophet Hosea told them in Hosea 4:1 to, *"Hear the word of the Lord, ye children of Israel: for the Lord hath a controversy with the inhabitants of the land, because there is no truth, nor mercy, nor knowledge of God in the land."* The more we know about God, the more we can understand the things of God.

There are things that we neither can nor ever understand about God, but when you know and learn about Him, God will reveal Himself to you. Not only to help us, but to help others that God will put in our pathways to help them know about God and His son Jesus Christ, who paid the ultimate price for a people who have either accepted, rejected or feel have no reason to believe in Him. Nevertheless, He did it for us all and all we should do is just trust in Him.

We trust in a God that can do anything but lie and fail, for God will never do either one of these things. Not only won't He do these things, rather when you do trust Him, you will be blessed. Psalms 40:4 says, *"Blessed is that man that maketh the Lord his trust, and respecteth not the proud, nor such as turn aside to lies."* Not only that, but He promises us in Psalms 84:12 that, *"O Lord of host, blessed is the man that trusteth in thee."* So, if God promises something, He will stand by it just because He is God. God never goes back on His word.

Yes, knowing God is to love Him, but how can you love unless you have trust? Because there are still those who say they love God, but they don't trust Him. It's true that to know God is to love Him, but moreso, when you really let Him into your life 100 percent, you will see that to know Him is to trust Him!

Be True

Philippians 4:8

"Finally, brethren, whatsoever things are true, whatsoever things are honest, whatsoever things are just, whatsoever things are pure, whatsoever things lovely, whatsoever things are of good report; if there be any virtue, and if there by any praise, think on these things."

Wow! What a list of mannerism, for a lack of a better word that we, as believers of God's word, are to be towards others. Not just in the literal sense, but in the physical sense as well. If we don't "walk the walk" while we "talk the talk", then the things that we do are not of God, but strictly for self. If you actually want to live the life God wants you to live, not only do you have to be true to yourself, but to God as well.

And what about being true? It's about being honest. And what about being honest has to do with this? Well, if you take that adjective which comes from the Latin word 'honos' meaning honor, a person that has honor would wish to be referred to as being honest. It's defined as "not given to lying, cheating, stealing, etc." These are the ways of many, not of God, because of the sinful nature of man. 1 Peter 2:12 tells us, *"Having your conversation honest among the Gentiles: that, whereas they speak against you as evildoers, they may by your good works, which they shall behold, glorify God in the day of visitation."*

Another definition is, "not characterized by falsehood or intent to mislead", because should we mislead people, we are not doing God's will. In 2 Corinthians 13:7, Paul says, *"Now I pray to God that ye do no evil; not that we should appear approved, but that ye should do that which is honest, though we be as reprobates."* A reprobate is a person in "the state of being morally depraved", and if you have depraved yourself of morals, then you have no honor. If there's no honor, then you cannot be honest with or to anyone, including God, for we are to praise and honor God to His glorification, and not ourselves.

There are other meanings to honest, but the most honest thing that you can ever do is this: if you have not taken God and His son Jesus Christ into your life, then bow down and ask God's forgiveness. Allow Jesus into your life so that you can do that is *"good and acceptable in the sight of God our Saviour"* (1 Timothy 2:3).

If you really want to be honest of anything, look back in and over your life and see who has been honest. Then you should not question yourself when you walk and talk with God. So, be true to do His work, true to do His ways, and true to be one in Christ Jesus and with the Holy Spirit leading and guiding you. Even in this sinful flesh, we can still believe in Jesus Christ be true!

Think

Psalms 19:14

"Let the words of my mouth, and the meditation of my heart, be acceptable in thy sight, O Lord, my strength, and my redeemer."

Many times we do things, whether they are in words, deeds or actions, without doing or using what God has given us. Even if it does or does not glorify God, we still have that process of thought. But the thoughts that we do have are to be for His glory, for without God, where would we be? *"Let the words of my mouth"* is a fine example of what we should watch, which are the words that we speak.

Job 9:20 tells us, *"If I justify myself, mine own mouth shall condemn me: if I say, I am perfect, it shall also prove me perverse."* There are times that we may speak things and it causes more trouble than intended. James 3:10 tells us, *"Out of the same mouth proceedeth blessing and crusing. My brethren, these things ought not so to be."* So let the Holy Spirit allow us to think about the words of our mouths.

"And the meditation of my heart,". Since God looks at our hearts in each and every thing we do, let us meditate in Him. Psalms 77:12 says that, *"I will meditate also of all thy work, and talk of thy doing."* God allows us to think of all the things He has done in our lives.

Not only that, but to also praise Him for all of His doings, for if we take credit for God's doings, He will not be exalted, glorified or praised. Our praise is what God desires from us more so than anything.

"Be acceptable in thy sight,". When we were young, we wanted to do things that were acceptable in the eyes of our parents, then as we aged, in the sight of our peers. But now that we have given our lives to Jesus, we want to do good as in 1 Timothy 2:3; *"For this is good and acceptable in the sight of God our Saviour;"*. We must remember that we are doing these things for God's glory and to be acceptable in His sight.

"O Lord, my strength,". We should always look to God as our strength, just as Moses said in Exodus 15:2; "The Lord is my strength and song, and he is become my salvation: he is my God, and I will prepare him an habitation; my father's God, and I will exalt him." It's by His grace that we are kept strong in Him. His praise on our lips is like a song and our safe place in times of trouble because only God alone can do and be all of these things to us.

"And my redeemer." Just as the angel said unto Joseph about Mary in Matthew 1:21; *"And she shall bring forth a son, and thou shalt call his name Jesus: for he shall save his people from their sins."* How it was going to be done is something Joseph did not know, but true to the angel's word, he indeed saved "his people from their sins". The way it was done was in total sacrifice.

Sometimes, we think we have it bad, but think about this: what if Christ did not lay down His life for us? Then where will we be? Think of His goodness and grace! Think of His mercy! Think!!

<u>Living By Faith</u>

Romans 1:17

Now, for a lot of us, this has to be perhaps the hardest thing to do. No matter how saved we have become or how long we have been saved, it can be very difficult. A lot of times, we just like to have it laid out in front of us so that all we need to do is connect the dots. That would be the simple way to do it, but it would not constitute faith. Now, the word 'constitute' means to be the substance or elements of; make up, compose. Hebrews 11:1 says, *"Now faith is the substance of things hoped for, the evidence of things not seen."* But still, we feel it's difficult.

A true example of us living in or by faith is given by Paul in his letter to Rome in Romans 1:17; *"For there in is the righteousness of God revealed from faith to faith: as it is written, the just shall live by faith"*. This is true faith, faith in God, but the sad part of this is the faith that we go by is in ourselves and not the faith we have in God. Even with that, we still struggle with it. We see in Matthew 9:21-22 about a woman's real faith, living in it and the reward that she reaped from it: *"For she said within herself, 'If I may but touch his garment, I shall be whole.' But Jesus turned about, and when he saw her, he said 'Daughter, be of good comfort; thy faith hath made thee whole.' And the woman was made whole from that hour."*

If that is not enough to show real faith, look at Matthew 9:27-29; *"And when Jesus departed thence, two blind men followed him, crying, and saying, 'Thou son of David, have mercy on us.' And when he was come into the house, the blind men came to him: and Jesus saith unto them, 'Believe ye that I am able to do this?' They said unto him, 'Yea Lord.' Then touched he their eyes, saying, 'According to your faith be it unto you.'"*

Just by this itself, we, as children of God, shall live by faith each and every day of our lives. Just because God blesses you the way He does, look at Matthew 5:45. You can see, *"That ye may be the children of your Father which is in heaven: for he maketh the sun to rise on the evil and on the good, and sendeth rain on the just and on the unjust".* But don't worry, for there is hope. In 1 John 1:9, we see that, *"If we confess our sins, he is faithful and just to forgive us our sins, and to cleanse us from all unrighteousness".*

But do you know who do live by faith? More than those who profess Christ? Homeless people, because a lot of times, they don't know from one day to the next what they will eat, where they will sleep or anything else.

Who would know more about homeless people than Jesus? In Matthew 8:20, he answered a scribe; "And Jesus saith unto him. *'The foxes have holes, and the birds of the air have nest; but the Son of man hath not where to lay his head.'"* The one who created it all did not have a home in His creation! Although heaven is his home, his flesh did not have a place to stay.

The sad thing is at times, we're just one paycheck away from being in that same spot. But like them, as long as we look to God and not ourselves, we will continue living by faith!

The Answer

1 Peter 3:15

"But sanctify the Lord God in your hearts: and be ready always to give an answer to every man that asketh you a reason of the hope that is in you in meekness and fear:"

The world as a whole is always searching for the answer to an unasked question by man's standard. But by God's standard, His answer is much better than ours, and by seeking Him in your life, it will be given to you. This is why the world always asks those who have taken the real answer into their lives.

Now, the word 'answer' comes from the Old English word *Andswarian*, which has an unknown meaning, but it has four definitions which would make it an intransitive verb, and five definitions that makes it a transitive verb. That in itself can be confusing, just as the disciples had been at times when Jesus has answered them in the form of parables. But here was *the answer* giving the answers to what man must do to live life correctly in the sight of God. The example that was given to us so that we may be able to live that life and keep His word in our hearts.

Whatever is in your heart will come out of your mouth, so that you can *"be ready always to give an answer to every man."* There are times when we think we have the answer, but it truly isn't. When it comes from God, it will be nothing else but right.

God has given each and every one of us who allows the Lord to be first in their lives the true answer to a sin-sick world that is always hungry for knowledge of one sort or another.

There was an NBA player who was known as The Answer, but like others, including Satan and those who don't accept Christ, they will know the real answer. Paul told the church of Philippi in Philippians 2:10-11; *"That at the name of Jesus every knee should bow, of things in heaven, and things in earth, and things under the earth; And that every tongue should confess that Jesus Christ is Lord, to the glory of God the Father."* But we being the wayward children that we are, we don't always give the correct answer.

So, when you look to God for any and everything in your life, always speak to Him in prayer and read His word. Through Christ, you will find that which you seek, and that will be the answer!

He Will Answer You

1 Thessalonians 5:24

"Faithful is he that calleth you, who also will do it."

Each and every one of us who accepted Jesus Christ, (and even those who have not) have a special gift. It's special because God gave it especially for you and nobody else can be able to use that gift like you, by you and but you so that God will be glorified. I cannot say may, because if you say may, then you would have question or doubt and God is not a God that puts doubt in his children. You're special because God really did make you that way and if nobody else has never said or told you that before, let me be the first to tell you, in Jesus' name, that you're special.

But think about it; if God took the time to make you, doesn't that make you special? You don't have to sing like Fred Hammond or teach like Noel Jones or do comedy like Jonathan Slocum. God has that one special gift or sometimes more than one to be used for the glory of God. And yes, you are special. You're special because your Father took the time to number every hair on your head, to design you especially to go thru the trials and tribulations of your life, to shape and mold you for the person that God has for you. He especially mapped out your life from start to finish; the good, bad and ugly of it, and God had put it there just so He will be glorified. You see, we co-exist within the realm of time, while God exists outside of time.

He can either slow it down or speed it up, but He will do it to His glory.

Special, which comes from the Latin word *species* meaning kind, is an adjective with a few definitions in which one of them is unique: exceptional. God has a unique work for us all to do, and with his Holy Spirit working through us, that work will be quite exceptional.

It is also defined as intimate; beloved, and that is how our relationship with God should be, but at times it isn't. "Faithful is he that calleth you". Think about it; God has called you to do a special work with your special gift that it will show others the way towards Him. In John 1:12, it says, *"But as many as received him, to them gave he power to become the sons of God, even to them that believe on his name:"*. Since He has called you, you have already been gifted for the task. Not only that, but you were given power to accomplish it as well.

So, as you sit, realize just how special God has made you. By using that gift to praise Him, we have to use the one gift that has been given to us all: prayer. We must use prayer to speak to our heavenly Father to do His will and guide us in how to use our special gift while staying in His word. When you do, He will answer you!

<u>What Are You Looking For?</u>

Psalms 27:8

"When thou sadist, 'Seek ye my face'; my heart said unto thee, 'Thy face, Lord, will I seek.'"

So many times, so many days, and sad to say, for so many years, we go about seeking many things and everything, but the one real thing we should seek is God. Once you seek God, you will have no desire to seek anything else. In Psalms 27:4, David tells us that, *"One thing have I desired of the Lord, that will I seek after; that I may dwell in the house of the Lord all the days of my life, to behold the beauty of the Lord, and to enquire in his temple."* You see, David had a mindset, and that mindset was giving glory unto God.

We don't have to be high-minded, sophisticated people to seek after God. If it were not for God's goodness, grace and mercy, along with the common sense He installed in us all, (even though we may not use it a lot) think of where you would be. In times of worship, praise, prayer and meditating in His word, we are actually seeking God, may it be directly or indirectly. You do not need status or title to do such, for we all are free to seek Him.

The word 'seek' comes from the Old English word *Secan*. It's a verb, meaning it describes action, and according to Isaac Newton's second law of motion, for every action, there is an equal and opposite reaction. So how does this pertain to it? Simply this: seek means to go in search of; look for, meaning the search is the action, and the discovery of such is the reaction.

Jesus even tells us in Matthew 6:33, *"But seek ye first the kingdom of God, and his righteousness; and all of these things shall be added unto you."* We should be doing what we can in seeking God, for He alone can help, hold, shape and mold us into the people that He wants us to be, giving Him honor, praise and glory to be His chosen vessels that were paid for with a price no man can ever match.

So, as we keep our minds, hearts and souls stayed and fixed on Jesus, even at times when things get rocky, they will be smoothed out all but soon enough. But ask yourself this question: if you are not seeking God, what are you looking for?

Real Faith

Matthew 9:20

Every day we go throughout our day with one sort of trial or tribulation or another. But no matter what has been thrown at us, we always have managed to *persevere*, defined as 'to persist in any purpose or enterprise; strive in spite of difficulties, etc.' just because we all have faith. Now there are people who feel that all they need is faith in themselves, but do I have news for you; those who have faith in those things, in the end, will only wind up on the bottom.

Paul tells us in Romans 12:3, *"For I say, through the grace given unto me, to every man that is among you, not to think of himself more highly than he ought to think; but to think soberly, according as God hath dealt to every man the measure of faith."* But we struggle with this honestly, because a lot of times we have more faith in things rather than God. When we wake up in the morning, we tend to have faith in the light switch to turn on the light, we have enough faith in the faucet to let water come out, we even have the nerve to have more faith in the pews that we sit in church than we do in the true and living God. However, this is what we should always have faith in such as the woman with the issue of blood.

In Matthew 9:20-21, it tells us, *"And, behold, a woman, which was diseased with an issue of blood twelve years, came behind him, and touched the hem of his garment: For she said within herself, If I but touch his garment, I shall be whole."*

Let's look at this for a moment, this woman had an infirmity and had it for quite some time. Luke 8:43 says, *"And a woman having an issue of blood twelve years, which had spent all her living upon physicians, neither could be healed of any."* So now, she is down to nothing, and a lot of times it's when we get to this point of our lives when we do things we normally don't do. A lot of times, it is done out of nothing more than sheer desperation. But this woman was desperate for the one thing that would be able to truly heal her and she had the faith to believe that it would be done.

How did she know this? Mark 5:27 lets us know that *"When she had heard of Jesus, came in the press behind, and touched his garment."* Just as I mentioned earlier, as we fight throughout the day, this woman had to fight through a crowd of people. A lot of times, people will be the one thing that will try to keep you away from your greatest blessing or will try to keep you from God and a deeper and better relationship with Jesus. She could not get to Him, so she had to come from behind, wishing to do nothing more than touch the invisible place of a visible God. This lets you know how strong her faith actually was, and in that same moment, she was made whole. This is what it means to really have real faith.

You Are Never Alone

John 8:29

"And he that sent me is with me: the Father hath not left me alone; for I do always those things that please him."

There are times when we (or we think) are all alone, whether it be in a traffic jam or a crowded sidewalk, often we do feel that we are alone. But Jesus tells us that we are not alone. No matter where we are, or where we may go, God is always with us. Therefore, you can never be alone. The word alone also means 'without equal; unique: unparalleled', and in each one of our lives, God should and shall stand alone in our lives. Because if He doesn't, we will put our focus on the wrong thing and not on the most single solitary thing that it should be on in the first place.

David in Psalms 139:7-10 tells us, *"Whither shall I go from thy spirit? Or whither shall I flee from thy presence? If I ascend up into heaven, thou art there: If I make my bed in hell, behold, thou art there. If I take the wings of the morning, and dwell in the uttermost parts of the sea; Even there shall thy hand lead me, and thy right hand shall hold me."* This lets you know that no matter where you may be, God is there for you.

This is why He is called Jehovah Shammah, which means the Lord is there, being omnipresent, meaning He is everywhere and anywhere at the same time. Remember, God is with you at all times, no matter how bright, no matter how dark.

No matter what storm, trial or tribulation that you're in, remember God is with you through it all and that you're never alone.

What Is Your Desire?

Psalms 27:4

"One thing have I desired of the Lord, that will I seek after; that I may dwell in the house of the Lord all the days of my life, to behold the beauty of the Lord, and to enquire in his temple."

Thoughts, goals, dreams and desires are things that each and every one of us has. Whether it is for good or evil, we have them all. The one thing we will touch on is desire, for we all have a desire to do something. Jesus gave up His life to fulfill His desire, that there will be a bridge to connect man to God. Desire is defined as a longing or craving, whether it be health, money, power etc, we desire of and for it. Sometimes, our desire can come from our hearts, and if it's within the heart then God can see if our desire is to His glory or not. There are times our desire overtakes our thoughts and can be made distorted, and when that happens, Satan has in one way or another founded himself into something that has nothing to do with God.

That's a desire of the flesh and it happened in Eden when the serpent spoke to Eve. He appealed to her desire in Genesis 3:6, *"And when the woman saw that the tree was good for food, and that it was pleasant to the eyes, and a tree to be desired to make one wise, she took of the fruit thereof, and did eat, and gave also unto her husband with her; and he did eat."*

This led to Adam and Eve being forced out of Eden.

Two reasons why we have to be careful of this type of thing: (1) Paul already lets us know in Romans 7:18, *"For I know that in me (that is, in my flesh,) dwelleth no good thing: for to will is present with me; but how to perform that which is good I find not."* Simply stating, unless He dwells in us (having the Holy Ghost) naturally we're not going to do anything good.

(2) Because Satan also has desires for us as well. Jesus tells us in Luke 22:31, *"And the Lord said, 'Simon, Simon, behold, Satan hath desired to have you, that he may sift you as wheat."* The word sift means to separate; distinguish, and what Satan wants to do is separate you from Christ and distinguish you as one of his own, not God's. But you know David had a desire, Satan has a desire and Jesus has a desire, so ask yourself, what is your desire?

How To Live Abundantly

Ephesians 3:20

"Now unto him that is able to do exceeding abundantly above all that we can ask or think, according to the power that worketh in us."

Isn't it great to know that there's someone who wishes nothing but the best for you? Just like the faithful parent that He is to do as much as they can for their children, God is like that with us. But before I continue, I'll let you know now, in order to live abundantly, it's not going to be easy nor will it be pretty because you will have to do God's will and way according to His purpose and plan.

The word abundantly comes from the word 'abundant' which comes from the Latin word *abundare*. The word abound comes from is existing in plentiful supply; ample. For where we, who are finite, God is infinite, because what we conceive or perceive, God can and will exceed!

Jesus tells us in John 10:10 that, *"The thief cometh not, but for to steal, and to kill, and to destroy: I am come that they might have life and that they might have it more abundantly."* You know that when it comes from God, it brings life and more than can be expected from any man. When we live abundantly, we shall sing praises to God as David did in Psalms 145:7. *"They shall abundantly utter the memory of thy great goodness, and shall say of thy righteousness."*

Give God what is deserving of Him for being able to live abundantly. But before we can live abundantly like God wants us to, Isaiah 55:7 says, *"Let the wicked forsake his way, and the unrighteous man his thoughts: and let return unto the Lord, and he will have mercy upon him; and to our God, for he will abundantly pardon."* Again, we have to turn our lives over to Christ to be able to live abundantly.

As I said earlier, we must live a life for God according to His will, way, purpose and plan. No matter what Satan throws at you, stay in the knowledge of Jesus Christ and look to Him for all that you need in life. That is the real way of living abundantly!

Where Is Your Refuge?

Psalm 46:1

"God is our refuge and strength, a very present help in trouble."

As we go through this adventure called life, we will partake in trials and tribulations, also known as storms, and with these storms, we must find what is known as refuge. The word refuge is composed of two Latin words: *re,* meaning 'backwards', and *fugere*, meaning 'to flee'.

In it's literal sense, to flee backwards is defined as:

1. **Shelter or protection**. Jesus tells us in John 14:2 that, *"In my father's house are many mansions: if it were not so, I would have told you. I go to prepare a place for you."* This lets us know that once we go into glory, we will not be homeless.
2. **One who, or that which shelters or protects**. In Matthew 8:20, it says *"And Jesus saith unto him, 'The foxes have holes, and the birds of the air have nests; but the Son of man hath not where to lay his head."* Even if we don't have a physical place, we know who will be a refuge for us all.
3. **A safe place; asylum**. David lets us know in Psalm 61:3 as he goes to God, *"For thou hast been a shelter for me, and a strong tower from the enemy."* It is in God that we are truly safe. So, my question to you is this: if you can't go to God, then where is your refuge?

How Are You Thinking?

Isaiah 55:8

"For my thoughts are not your thoughts, neither are your ways my ways, saith the Lord."

In this, God is letting us know the difference of how He thinks and how we think, which is amazing that we cannot begin to imagine. But we have to be careful of how we think because Paul tells us in 1 Corinthians 10:12 that, *"Wherefore let him that thinketh he standeth take heed lest he fall."*

The word 'thought' is the act or process of using the mind actively and deliberately, or meditation meaning to engage in continuous and contemplative thought or cogitation, which is careful consideration. That is what we all have to do with all of our thoughts, for we have thoughts that are good which would give God glory and we have evil thoughts that gives place to Satan. Paul also lets know in Philippians 4:8, *"Finally, brethren, whatsoever things are true, whatsoever things are honest, whatsoever things are just, whatsoever things are pure, whatsoever things are lovely, whatsoever things are of good report; if there be any virtue, and if there be any praise, think on these things."*

I really don't believe there's more to say but I'm sad to say there is because a lot of times, since we are flesh, Satan has a way of sneaking into our thoughts. We must be on guard because Solomon tells us in Proverbs 23:7,

"For as he thinketh in his heart, so is he: Eat and drink, saith he to thee; but his heart is not with thee." So, if your thoughts are not in tune with God, then how are you thinking?

A Minus Is A Plus

Hebrews 11:6

"These are the times that try men's soul." This is a quotation by Thomas Paine in his newspaper, "The Crisis", which was written during a revolution, the American Revolution, when some of our forefathers fought for political freedom. Today, we as the children of God fight for spiritual freedom, not just our own but those who desire to have it.

But instead of saying "men's soul", we can say, "our faith", which the Devil, as well as the world, tries to discourage and defeat. Moreso than anything, Satan wants to take one very important thing from us: faith. For as long as we have faith in a prayer answering God, we have all that we need, and we do need faith. Hebrews 11:6 tells us, *"But without faith it is impossible to please him: for he cometh to God must believe that he is, and that he is a rewarder of them that diligently seek him."*

As long as we have faith and believe God, we can achieve. Satan wishes to say words to us like can't and won't, but stop and compare them to two other words: can and won. You will see a big difference in them, not just in terms of definition, but in spelling. The only difference in their spelling is the letter "T", and Jesus hung from that "T" to give us the spiritual freedom that we need.

Satan wants to deceive and discourage you. When he tells you that you can't, you can tell him what Paul wrote in Philippians 4:13,

"I can do all things through Christ which strengtheneth me." And when he says you won't, you can take off that "T" to make it 'won', because 1 John 4:4 says that *"Ye are of God, little children, and have overcome them: because greater is he that is in you, than he that is in the world."* Since Jesus died for the remission of our sins to allow God in our lives, we've achieved the biggest victory in our lives, and in that, a minus is a plus!

God's Alphabet

What do we do for God? Well, first we:

(A)ccept Him into our lives.

(B)elieve in and on Him.

(C)onfess who God is.

(D)elight in God, according to Proverbs 37:4.

(E)ndure in the race.

Have (F)aith always in God.

(G)lorify God to the highest.

(H)umble yourself, according to 1 Peter 5:6.

(I)dentify to yourself that you're God's child.

The (J)ust shall live by faith.

For He is the (K)ing of kings.

And (L)ords of lords.

The (M)ighty one in our lives.

For (N)othing is impossible for God.

(O)perate under God's power.

(P)ray always.

(Q)uench any hold the devil has on you through Christ.

Jesus was (R)esurrected for our salvation.

For Jesus is our (S)avior.

Our strong (T)ower, according to Psalms 61:3.

(U)nify yourself with Christ.

Be able to praise God in your (V)alley.

For God is (W)onderful.

To the world we are the (X)eno ones in a xeno land.

He is your (Y)eshua.

And serve Christ with (Z)eal.

Even The Bad Is Good

Genesis 50:20

"But as for you, ye thought evil against me; but God meant it unto good, to bring to pass as it is this day, to save much people alive."

There are times when bad things happen to us, whether they were caused by Satan or one of his agents. Even still, God allowed you to go through such times as those to prove true what Paul had said in Romans 8:28. *"And we know that all things work together for good to them that love the God, to them who are the called according to his purpose."* We were called by God for the purpose of bringing the lost to the saving grace and knowledge of Christ Jesus with whatever gift or gifts that God has put into us, for His glory and not our own!

Even in this scripture, which tells us that Joseph's brothers thought that Joseph was going to get revenge against them. Instead, Joseph took the high road and showed them two attributes of God that we know so well: compassion and forgiveness/mercy.

It reminds me of two stories that God brought to my remembrance, which are "The 4 bad D's versus the 4 good D's" and "The 5th bad D versus the 5th good D", where it speaks of five bad things in my life, or at least at that time, I thought were bad but God showed me otherwise. The five bad were (1) Death (2) Departure (3) Divorce (4) Destruction and (5) Despair. God had shown me the good in these bad times in three points.

(1) Destruction and Departure. The reason why God caused these things to happen was due to they were more important than (a) having a relationship with God and (b) having a real friend like Jesus. God told Moses in Exodus 34:14, *"For thou shalt worship no other god: for the Lord, whose name is Jealous, is a jealous God:"*. As long as you put God first, you will not see destruction or feel His departure.

(2) Divorce. The life I led caused it, but due to His grace and mercy, as God told Judah in Joel 2:25, *"And I will restore to you the years that the locust hath eaten, the cankerworm, and the caterpillar, and the palmerworm, my great army which I sent among you."* God had restored my marriage, home and children in order to live a better life for Him.

(3) Death and Despair. These are perhaps the hardest things anyone can go through in life. They will be upsetting due to the sudden changes, but Psalms 30:5 tells us that, *"For his anger endureth but a moment; in his favor in life: weeping may endure for a night, but joy cometh in the morning."* So, when things look bad but they're not, remember that even the bad is good.

Call It By Name

John 11:43

"And when he thus had spoken, he cried with a loud voice. 'Lazarus, come forth.'"

We all have a voice that God desires for us to use. When we're in His house, or wherever we may be, He would like for us to give Him praise for what He has done in our lives. Whether it be good, bad or indifferent, it's still good to praise Him. 1 Thessalonians 5:18 instructs us, *"In every thing give thanks: for this is the will of God in Christ Jesus concerning you."*

We know that there are things in our lives that we have to speak out of our lives, but on the other hand, God has pre-destinate things that we can speak into our lives as well. God has a purpose and a plan in the lives of each and every believer. Whether they by young or old, rich or poor, man or woman, black or white, God has a set or people designed just for you to bring to the saving knowledge of Jesus Christ because with Christ, there's life.

Jesus had to be careful about who he called out, for had He just said 'come forth', every grave would have been empty. All He needed was just one to show them who He is. Solomon tells us in Proverbs 18:21 that, *"Death and life are in the power of the tongue: and they that it shall eat of the fruit thereof."*

So, the fruit of your tongue shall depend strictly on you. We are to be aware of how we speak, because the things that we speak could either be our greatest blessings or our worst adversities. James 3:10 says that *"Out of the same mouth proceedeth blessings and cursing. My brethren, these things ought not so to be."* Therefore, we're to be careful of what we say.

Solomon also tells us in Proverbs 14:25, *"A true witness deliverth souls; but a deceitful witness speaketh lies."* So, the things that we say to the people of the world should be words that will allow them to receive the Savior, and careful not just in our talk but our walk as well. What we don't say says the most about us and we should be that true witness for the Lord. And you cannot do this under your own power, for if you try that way, you may have more trouble than you have bargained for. So, in anything that you do, do it under the anointing of the Holy Ghost, and then in Jesus' name, you will be able to call it by name.

The Liquid of Life

Hebrews 9:12

Liquid is the one thing that makes up a large percentage of our body weight; the one thing that sustains life in the human body. But there is a liquid that not only allows our physical life to continue, but our spiritual life as well, and that liquid is the blood of Jesus, which was shed on Calvary's cross for our sins past, present and future.

Hebrews 9:12 tells us, *"Neither by the blood of goats and calves, but by his own blood he entered in once into the holy place, having obtained eternal redemption for us."* The only way sins were forgiven at that time were by sacrifices of animals and their blood shedding. Now, there is a different route to take, and you don't have to get your hands messy, nor do you have to sit in a booth and tell them to a person who will intercede for you. Jesus has already done that job for you with His death, burial and resurrection, when He ascended to be with God the Father to intercede for us and our sins. We must accept the fact that He died for our sins and believe in our hearts that He did this very important job for a very important person: *you.* No matter what you or what the devil tries to put into your mind, you are always important to God, even when you don't feel important to yourself.

Liquid is one of the three main substances that we have here on earth, but the liquid that we're speaking of is composed of two things: blood and water. John 19:34 states, as Jesus hung on the cross, *"But one of the soldiers with a spear pierced his side, and forthwith came there out blood and water.*" We know that He rose from the dead and sits on the right hand of God, but it was by His death that we were able to receive the liquid of life.

How To Mend a Broken Heart

Psalms 119:2

"Blessed are they that keep his testimonies, and that seek him with the whole heart."

Let me begin by asking a question: what was it that killed Jesus? When I say this, I'm meaning from a spiritual sense. Sin is what killed Jesus. From a physical sense, it was from a number of things due to the crucifixion, but from an emotional sense, Jesus really died from this: a broken heart.

I can honestly make this statement for these two reasons that God revealed to me; (1) Since Jesus is God in the flesh, He was able to see how His children treated Him and His word. Like any parent when your children hurt you, it can break your heart so you can imagine how Jesus felt. (2) Since Jesus is the Son, God had to turn His back on Jesus because of the sin that He had to take on in order to be the passageway to God. He did not obtain an answer to His question, according to Matthew 27:46, *"And about the ninth hour Jesus cried with a loud voice, saying, 'Eli, Eli, lama sabachthani?' that is to say, My God, my God, why hast thou forsaken me?"*

I'm sure that because His Father turned away from Him, it broke His heart. A broken heart is perhaps the hardest thing that a person can get over, but just as anything else in life, it takes time. But that's just one ingredient. The one thing that we would really need to cure a broken heart would be love. I'm not talking about any particular love, I'm speaking of a love that no human on the face of this earth can be able to give to you. This love can only come from one place: GOD!!!! Because how much love can one person give by putting the only child He ever had up for a sacrifice of all evil that we've ever committed? God has and did this.

If it's not a good enough example of how much He loves you, just stand in front of a mirror and hold your arms out wide. Even that is not large enough. Stand at that same mirror, walk towards it as you would be walking towards God taking you into His arms. He can and will cure your broken life, due to the sins that we've all partaken before receiving Christ. The broken dreams that only God can repair, and more importantly, it's truly God's love that is the main thing that can mend a broken heart!

If: Small But Mighty

Romans 10:9

"That if thou shalt confess with thy mouth the Lord Jesus and shalt believe in thine heart that God hath raised him from the dead, thou shalt be saved."

This is a scripture that has been quoted time and time again to inform people of the benefits of, not just salvation, but having Christ in your life. Now, the word 'if' comes from the Greek word *ei*, meaning a primary particle of conditionality. It is also referred to as a conditional blessing, meaning that when you carry out the first part, you will receive the blessing that is contained in it.

There are two letters to the word 'if'. The first letter "I", is the ninth letter of the alphabet, and the number nine represents first fruits. Now, the second letter "F" is the sixth letter of the alphabet, and the number six represents man. So, it's literal meaning is "first fruits of man". In this piece, you will be receiving the fruit of the Holy Spirit starting to work in your spirit.

There's a lot of mighty but small things and people, like Napoleon, who was under five feet tall but still managed to conquer most of Europe. Just as Jesus had told the parable of the mustard seed in Matthew 13:31-32, *"Another parable put he forth unto them, saying, The kingdom of heaven is like a grain of mustard seed, which a man took, and sowed in his field: Which indeed is the least of all seeds: but when it is grown, it is the greatest among herbs, and becometh a tree, so that the birds of the air come and lodge in the branches thereof."* So, as you go and grow in the knowledge of Jesus Christ, you will be just like that word 'if'. You will be small, but mighty!

God's Acceptance

Jeremiah 1:7-8

"But the Lord said unto me, 'Say not, I am a child: for thou shalt go to all that I shall send thee, and whatsoever I command thee thou shalt speak. Be not afraid of their faces: for I am with thee to deliver thee,' saith the Lord."

As a child, Jeremiah had received the one thing that we need from God other than salvation, which is acceptance. In some form or another, it's what we look for or seek from parents, spouses, mentors, etc. We wish to have acceptance so that we fit in. Acceptance from man is fleeting, but the real acceptance that we should seek or look for comes from God, or we will be like empty vessels waiting for a temporary filling.

When we have the acceptance of God, we will be filled because we seek after the righteousness of God. Jesus said in his sermon on the mount in Matthew 5:6, *"Blessed are they which do hunger and thirst after righteousness; for they shall be filled."* When we are filled with His righteousness, acceptance is no longer an issue, but an established fact. When He sees that righteousness, He sees himself. He's pleased and accepts what He sees.

So, when we want real righteousness, we should do what David said in Psalms 19:14, *"Let the words of my mouth, and the meditation of my heart, be acceptable in thy sight, O Lord, my strength, and my redeemer."* Because remember, man's acceptance is good, but the real acceptance that we need is God's acceptance!

Know The Purpose

Romans 8:28

"And we know that all things work together for good to them that love God, to them who are the called according to His purpose."

So many times and so many days, God always has a work for us, but because of our own stubbornness and the distractions of Satan and his demons, we don't realize what it is and will not know unless we attune ourselves to what God has for us to do. And how do we do that? Through prayer, fasting and mostly reading and learning. Once we dwell in God, he will dwell in us and we will know what our purpose is in this world.

Those who are called to do God's will are able to carry out His purpose and plan that He has for this world, that will be able to reach, teach and bring those that are in the darkness into the marvelous light of Jesus Christ. And since, we are called for His purpose and not our own. If it's for our own purpose, it will not succeed. God will not bring it to pass.

Purpose is a noun which comes from two old French words: *'pro'*, meaning *forth* and *'poser'*, meaning *to put*, literally meaning to put forth. That is what God wants us to do; to put forth our best so that in turn, He will give the best to His children like any other loving father. Purpose is an idea or ideal kept before the mind as an end of effort or action, and the idea of re-establishing a relationship between man and God was

Jesus Christ. 1 John 3:8 tells us, *"He that committeth sin is of the devil; for the devil sinneth from the beginning. For this purpose the Son of God was manifested, that he might destroy the works of the devil."* When we follow Christ, we commit ourselves to destroy sin, and when that is done, we have the devil out of yet another place and put God there that He can manifested.

It is also a particular thing to be effected or attained. Paul informs Timothy about his call from God to let him know in 2 Timothy 1:9, *"Who hath saved us, and called us with a holy calling, not according to our works, but according to his own purpose and grace, which was given us in Christ Jesus before the world began"*, which lets us know when our purpose and lay out is, so that it will be attained. So, when you go before God to find out your purpose, trust in Him and He will allow you to see the purpose in this life and you will know the purpose.

S.A.F.E.

Psalms 57:1

"Be merciful unto me, O God, be merciful unto me: for my soul trusteth in thee: yea, in the shadow of thy wings will I make my refuge, until these calamities be overpast."

This is how David felt as he fled from Saul, and he asked God to do the one thing that only God can do. Although your mom and dad can do it, they can't do it like God. To have this type of security is something we all really like to have, and God will keep you that way. There are four points that I'll give you to be safe.

First, we have "S", and Moses explains to us in Deuteronomy 33:29, *"Happy art thou, O Israel: who is like unto thee, O people saved by the Lord, the shield of thy help, and who is the word of thy excellency! and thine enemies shall be found liars unto thee; and thou shalt tread upon their high places."* Because God is our shield and our sword, we feel safe.

Second, is "A". Jesus tells us in John 15:7, *"If you abide in me, and my words abide in you, ye shall ask what ye will, and it shall be done unto you."* And as long as we abide in the love of Jesus Christ, we will be safe.

Third, there's "F". Paul tells us in 1 Thessalonians 5:24, *"Faithful is he that calledth you, who also will do it."* When you are faithful in the things of God, you will be safe.

Fourth, we go to "E", where Moses says in Psalms 90:2, *"Before the mountains were brought forth, everlasting to everlasting, thou art God."* When you're in the everlasting arms of God, you are safe.

With all of these things, (1) Your sword and shield (2) Simply abide (3) Be faithful and (4) Stay in the everlasting power of God, you will always be safe.

It's All Good

1 Thessalonians 5:18

"In everything give thanks: for this is the will of God In Christ Jesus concerning you."

There are times in our lives when we don't want to give God glory for one reason or another. We, who are the sons and daughters of God, should give the Lord that which He deserves, because of what He has brought us not just out of, which should demand praise, but through. For if you just sit for a good two seconds and think about what He did for not just this day but even as you read this, I'm sure that the Holy Ghost can get a hold of you and can see why it's all good.

He brought you into a new day, a day that is filled with hope. We have the hope of God as He stretches out His hand of protection over us, a day that was not promised to us as in Job 12:10. It says, *"In whose hand is the soul of every living thing, and the breath of all mankind."*

Because God Holds your very breath, it's not to be taken for granted nor think you have control of your life, for only God knows the day and hour. God is in control of all things, and since He is, one thing we should do is, as it's written in 1 Peter 3:17, *"Honour all men. Love the brotherhood. Fear God. Honor the king."* When it's done to His glory, it's all good.

A day of victory that you can and have over the devil, as long as you are stayed and prayed up by the grace and mercy given by God. Moses said in Exodus 33:19, *"And he said, 'I will make all my goodness pass before thee, and I will proclaim the name of the Lord before thee; and will be gracious to whom I will be gracious, and will show mercy on whom I will shew mercy.'"* That's when we show the grace and mercy of God towards others. Then, God will do the same to us, and in that, it's all good.

And so, as we continue to keep our hope in God, know that our victory, life, breath, grace and mercy comes from God and to stay in the will of God. No matter what comes before us, we can always give thanks to God because we know that it's all good!

Be There

Hebrews 13:5

"Let your conversation be without covetousness; and be content with such things as ye have: for he hath said, 'I will never leave thee, nor forsake thee.'"

This has to be one of the biggest reassurances that God has ever given us, to let us know that He will be there for us no matter what. It doesn't matter if we are up, down, weak, strong, happy, sad, smart or ignorant, God will be there for us. When we're up, we know as in Psalms 33:3 to *"Sing unto him a new song; play skillfully with a loud noise."* When we're down, we should remember what Paul said in Galatians 6:9, *"And let us not be weary in well doing: for in due season we shall reap, if we faint not."*

In times of weakness, we need to remember Isaiah 40:31, *"But they that wait upon the Lord shall renew their strength; they shall mount up with wings as eagles; they shall run, and not be weary; And they shall walk and not faint."* And when we're strong, we know like Paul did in Philippians 4:13 that, *"I can do all things through Christ which strengtheneth me."*

When we're happy, we let people know what was said in Philippians 4:4, that we *"Rejoice in the Lord always: and again I say, Rejoice."* And while we're sad, we are to know that in Psalms 30:5, *"For his anger endureth but a moment; in his favour is life: weeping may endure for a night, but joy cometh in the morning."*

When we're smart, we should remember 1 Corinthians 2:11, *"For what man knoweth the things of a man, save the spirit of man which is in him? even so the things of God knoweth no man, but the Spirit of God."* And even when we're ignorant in our sins, we know in Romans 5:8, *"But God commendeth his love toward us, in that, while we were yet sinners, Christ died for us."*

The reason why we know that he's there is because His name is also Jehovah-Shammah, meaning 'The Lord is There'. He is omnipresent, being anywhere and everywhere. He is where He is needed and not neglecting any of us at the same time. So, remember that when you have a proper relationship with God and are in need of Him, trust in Him and He will be there!

Give and Take

Matthew 16:25-26

"For whosoever will save his life shall lose it: and whosoever will lose his life for my sake shall find it. For what is a man profited, if he shall gain the whole world, and lose his own soul? or what shall a man give in exchange for his soul?"

Save, gain and profit also lose and exchange. These are the things that we do today; we save only to lose it in some form or another. There are times we profit from "a good day", and at the same time, turn into "a bad day". It's just a matter of how your day would be. But then again, you can always make an exchange, provided it's worth exchanging, because everything that is exchanged is worth being exchanged.

Take for example, the sin and iniquity we had in our lives and gave it to God, and in return He gave us the covering of His son's blood. Those who read God's word quite well know that we have what is known as The Great Commission, but before that, we had 'The Great Exchange', in which we traded condemnation for eternal life by our confession and belief of Jesus Christ. Christ gave His life so that we may have life and to let others know of that life.

Exchange means the act of giving or receiving one thing as equivalent for another, but every now and then, we give up one thing, and in return we gain something better. We felt at one point or another in life we gave up something we thought was important, and in return, God gave us something better to serve and glorify Him. He takes praise and gives blessings. He takes doubts and gives us hope. He takes darkness and gives us light. He takes sorrow and gives us joy. He exchanges the stumbling blocks that Satan puts in our pathway and makes them the building blocks of our faith. He exchanges our tragic times and makes them times of triumph. But mostly, he exchanges the lies of Satan for the reality of God's truth. In John 8:32, Jesus said, *"And ye shall know the truth, and the truth shall make you free."*

So, when you really think about it, this life with all the things we go through is not bad at all, because all that it really comes down to is nothing more than give and take!

What Would Jesus Do?

John 15:5

"I am the vine, ye are the branches. He that abideth in me, and I in him, the same bringeth forth much fruit: for without me ye can do nothing."

This title seems to be the most asked question of our present time and we ask it for several reasons; some as a tool of reason, some as a means of escape, while others use it to look "right", not just in the eyes of men, but God as well. But the only way we can truly answer that question is when we are abiding in Him and He is abiding in us. You see, the word abide means to continue in a place; to remain. But the question is this: How can Christ abide in us if we're not wishing to abide in the type of life He wishes for us to live?

Paul tells us in Romans 7:18, *"For I know that in me (that is, in my flesh) dwelleth no good thing: for to will is present with me; but to perform that which is good I find not."* The way to answer that is quite simple, since we wish to know of our heavenly Father and the things He can do, not just in our lives, but in the lives of others.

But for you to do that, you should (1) Accept, believe and confess that Jesus Christ as Lord and Savior in your life, (2) Learn to speak to our heavenly Father, because believe it or not, He wishes to hear what you have to say, and the way to do that is by spending time in prayer with Him. (3) Learn of Him through His word, because in it there is no lie within it.

These are the basics, but it's the basics that make everything so much better, and in time, you will know what Jesus would do.

Sadness to Sweetness

Isaiah 61:3

"To appoint unto them that mourn in Zion, to give unto them beauty for ashes, the oil of joy for mourning, the garment of praise for the spirit of heaviness; that they might be called trees of righteousness, the planting of the Lord, that he might be glorified."

This is to let us know that all we do, when it's to honor and give glory to God, will never be unrewarded because He is not that type of God. No matter how bad things are, regardless of your poor choices, remember that God is sovereign, for things that have caused you the most pain can bring you the greatest joy. The Bible has reminded us time and again of those who have been in situations so sad that only a sovereign God could make it sweet. Psalms 121:5 tells us that, *"The Lord is thy keeper: the Lord is thy shade upon thy right hand."* And there is no one else that can keep you the way God can.

Sovereign means possessing supreme excellence or efficacy, to remind us that God is supreme and will always be excellent in everything that He does in our lives. So, remember one and all to continue walking in Christ, because before you know, you will move from sadness to sweetness.

What A Fool Believes

Psalms 53:1

"The fool hath said in his heart, 'There is no God'.
Corrupt are they, and have done abominable iniquity:
there is none that doeth good."

It's amazing what's in the hearts of some and what's not in others, but to say that there is no God is insane. How can you doubt the existence of the One who created this world, gives you breath to breathe, a mouth to speak of His glory, a heart to sing His praises and a mind that thinks of His goodness? It's sad that people not only say it, but believe and swear on it.

People that feel that way have iniquity in their hearts, but Psalms 119:11 tells us, *"Thy word have I hid in mine heart, that I might not sin against thee."* That word, which is God's word, is the one thing that should be in our hearts so that we can do His will according to His purpose and plan that He has for us in our lives. Because a heart that has iniquity cannot be used by God.

Because we are human, we don't do good naturally, for there is no real good in us but the goodness that God places in our hearts. What we can do is this: show this world the true and living God, and by this, man will not believe what a fool believes.

Is It Worth It?

Matthew 16:26

"For what is a man profited, if he shall gain the whole world, and lose his soul? or what shall as man give in exchange for his soul?"

There are many times that people actually feel that what we do here is worth all that we go through. We wish not to go through anything unpleasant in our lives, especially when we desire to live a life for God. All of the pain, heartache, sorrow and so many other things we feel, we have to think, is it in vain or what?

Paul tells us in 2 Thessalonians 3:13, *"But ye, brethren, be not weary in well doing."* It's going to pay off for all of the trials and tribulations which we go through in the body of Christ, whether it be as a group or individually. It's for our growth in Jesus and to help others to grow in Him as well. People only see the end results of what people have become, such as T.D. Jakes, Jackie McClellan, Joyce Meyer and others who had poor beginnings but rose to be who they are. I'm sure there were times they have felt like we did, but God kept them, and just like He did with them, so shall He do so with you.

It's not bad to have things, but don't let things have you and take you away from the giver of all things in your life. If you don't believe me ask yourself this question: when you have everything and anything you ever want or need and you have not Him as Lord and Savior in your life, or having a happy and healthy relationship with Jesus Christ, is it worth it?

The Power of Forgiveness

Colossians 1:14

"In whom we have redemption through his blood, even the forgiveness of sins."

Forgiveness; a word that holds so much and yet can do so much in the life of a person. It can make a weak man strong, a foolish man wise and a great man greater still, and all from a single act, word or deed of forgiveness. Where indeed can just one thing do so much? But before we go there, we have to start with the word itself.

Forgiveness is a noun and a supplement of the word 'forgive', which comes from the old English word *'forgiefan'*, and is defined as a disposition to forgive. Thus adding the blood of Christ to our unqualified resumes allows us to be put in a position that we would be able to obtain anything possible. We can act as well as react to forgiveness and we can accept or reject it, but it's best to accept it just as Saul did on Damascus road. Jesus said in Acts 26:18, *"To open their eyes, and to turn them from darkness to light, and from the power of Satan unto God, that they may receive forgiveness of sins and inheritance among them which are sanctified by faith that is in me."*

Paul makes it quite plain for us when he wrote in Ephesians 1:7 that Christ, *"In whom we have redemption through his blood, the forgiveness of sins, according to the riches of his grace."*

And by that single act of love and grace, Jesus has shown us and will allow us all to truly know and bestow to others this real power of and from God: The power of forgiveness!

Can You See Me Now?

1 John 4:20

"If a man say, I love God, and hateth his brother, he is a liar: for he that loveth not his brother whom he hath seen, how can he love God whom he hath not seen?"

Sight. What a precious gift, yet we take it for granted for the most part, and for the most, we take our faith in God the same way. Too many times, God does so many things that are "under the radar". We take it all for granted and don't even take a second to show how much we appreciate the moment of God just being God.

The word sight comes from the old English word *'gesiht'*, which has many definitions: one being the act or fact of seeing, that which is seen; a view as well as others. But can we see God? From a physical standpoint, the answer is no. John 1:18 tells us, *"No man hath seen God at any time; the only begotten Son, which is in the bosom of the Father, he hath declared him."*

But when we as followers of Christ show His love, this world can see Him through us. The only way that can happen is by being in right relationship with God and knowing Him for yourself. Jesus tells us in John 14:7, *"If ye had known me, ye should have known my Father also: and from henceforth ye know him, and have seen him."* And that's when we feel that God can truly say, "Can you see me now?"

Are You a Servant?

Philippians 2:7

"But made himself of no reputation, and took upon him the form of a servant, and was made in the likeness of men:"

The world is truly fascinated about two things: (1) the existence and belief of God and, (2) that someone who had so much would be willing to give it up for us. Even the Bible is amazed by this according to Psalms 144:3 when David asks, *"lord, what is man, that thou takest knowledge of him! or the son of man, that thou makest account of him!"*, that he was willing to be a servant just for us, and yet the world just doesn't understand.

The word has a few meanings to it. It's the root word to the word 'serve', which comes from the Latin word *'servus'*, meaning slave. Although we may feel like one on our jobs, we can be an example of Christ there as well. But if you stop and think about it, being a servant isn't bad at all, because after all, two of the greatest men in the Bible were slaves: Paul and Daniel.

Let's start with Paul with all of the adversity that he had went through after receiving his true assignment from God. He explains himself in 1 Corinthians 9:19. In spite of all of his knowledge and stature, he said, *"For though I be free from all men, yet have I made myself servant unto all, that I might gain the more."* He was doing the same thing Jesus had done; being submissive in order for the greater one to come out.

In Daniel's case, even though he served God truthfully and faithfully, it was because of this he was placed in a den of lions to be devoured. But in Daniel 6:20, King Darius was calling for Daniel after spending the evening with the lions; *"And when he came to the den, he cried with a lamentable voice unto Daniel: and the king spake and said to Daniel, 'O Daniel, servant of the living God, is thy God, whom thou servest continually, able to deliver thee from the lions?"*

Not only had Daniel answered him and his foes were pushed into the lion's den and eaten immediately, but Darius had issued a decree for all the people in the kingdom to worship God. We know we cannot compare ourselves to these men, but we look within ourselves and ask ourselves this question: are you a servant?

The Cost

Luke 14:28

"For which of you, intending to build a tower, sitteth not down first and counteth the cost, whether he have sufficient to finish it?"

Everything and anything that we may say or do ultimately has a cost to it; whether it be a tank of gasoline, a kind gesture or even an insult, there is a cost to it. Some may be necessary, others may not, but regardless of the results of the actions we take or replace to take, there lies the cost. Just as Adam knew in Genesis 2:17; *"But of the tree of the knowledge of good and evil, thou shalt not eat of it: for in the day that thou eatest thereof thou shalt surely die."* This would be the cost of disobedience, but it falls under the principal of cost and effect: it costed him and Eve to leave the Garden of Eden and effected the earth with sin.

But just as the first Adam caused sin to enter the world, the last "Adam" was going to go through the cost, because He said in John 10:15, *"As the Father knoweth me, even so know I the Father: and I lay down my life for the sheep."* Jesus knew that once He gave up the physical life and that once we believe, our eternal life would be set and we would be in glory. To know the grace and mercy of Jesus Christ, we all have to experience the cost in our lives.

Forsaken: The Loneliest Feeling

Mark 15:34

Forsaken; does anybody really, truly and honestly know how it feels to be forsaken? We may think we do, but if we really look at everything from an overall view, we don't. We really don't, but there is one who does: Jesus Christ. Yes, the same one that we confess, love and adore knows the true feeling of being forsaken.

You ask how can He, being the Son of God, know what that feels like? If you look at Mark 15:34 when He took on the sins of the world, it says, *"And at the ninth hour Jesus cried with a loud voice, saying, 'Eloi, Eloi, lama sabachthani?' which is being interpreted, 'My God, My God, why has thou forsaken me?'"* He could not even glance upon Jesus because of all the sin that was upon him; the sins that were done at that time, the sins that would happen in this present time, and even after we are gone, the sins of future generations.

Forsaken is not something that can be taken lightly by any means. It's harsh, very, very harsh. Forsaken comes from the word 'forsake', which is from an old English word *'forsucan'*, which means to repudiate or deny. In other words, when Jesus took our dirt, God had to deny Him. When you see this, can you really look at yourself and feel that way? Sometimes we do after a loved one is taken away, a breakup, even a divorce. There are so many things that can be relevant to that, but even then, it's only for a short time. Even David, the one after God's own heart, had been there in Psalms 22:1 as he prayed, *"My God, My God, why hast thou forsaken me? why art thou so far from helping me, and from the words of my roaring?"* But despite it all, David also lets us know in Psalms 37:25 that, *"I have been young, and now am old; yet have I not seen the righteous forsaken, nor his seed begging bread."*

I could go on, but I feel now that you know that despite any and everything in life, you will not know, because you have a Savior who went through it for you. Forsaken: the loneliest feeling.

Despite Your Troubles

Job 14:1

"Man that is born of a woman is of few days, and full of trouble."

No matter how we look at things in life, you can be sure that trouble will rear its head towards us. But the question isn't what to do about it, but rather how do you face it? We have to face it with everything else that happens in life because, believe it or not, some trouble is good for us to grow in life. There are times when trouble makes life stink, but just like manure, it can help us grow better and stronger.

Trouble comes from the Latin word '*turba*', meaning crowd, which goes to show you why when there is a crowd, most of the time there is trouble. But even in the midst of trouble, God does quite a few things. Here we will see three of them.

First, he can hide us as in Psalms 9:9, *"The Lord also will be a refuge for the oppressed, a refuge in times of trouble."* Second, he will save you when you call upon Him as in Psalms 34:6, *"This poor man cried, and the Lord heard him, and saved him out of all his troubles."* And third, he will comfort you as Paul wrote in 2 Thessalonians 1:7, *"And to you who are troubled rest with us, when the Lord Jesus shall be revealed from heaven with his mighty angels."* So, the best thing we can and should do is not to worry or be concerned because God will stand and be with you, despite your troubles.

The 5 E's

Enrich- To desire the richness of God's word.

Encourage- To inspire with God's word.

Endure- To march on in God's word.

Edify- To feel the benefits of God's word.

Excellence- To see the beauty of God's word.

The 5 Men of the 5 E's

Enrich is *Solomon*, who was enriched in not only riches and land but wisdom as well.

Endure is *Job*, who despite death, illness and loss of finances he never thought otherwise not to look anywhere else but to God.

Encourage is *Peter*, who even after he denied Jesus three times as Christ said he would, he regained the courage to preach the word of God with no fear.

Edify is *David* for with the Psalms that he wrote shows what joy God's word has for us.

Excellence is *Paul* despite being imprisoned, he was still able to tell as well as show how beautiful God's word actually is.